UNDERSTANDING
AND
OVERCOMING
ADDICTIONS
MADE EASY

DREW SYKES

ISBN# 978-0-9810561-8-0
COPYRIGHT 2016
DREW SYKES

DISCLAIMER

INTRODUCTION

THIS BOOK is primarily about overcoming/addictions and other bad habits. This book may also be helpful in dealing with some mental health issues. During my research I discovered most recovering addicts have an element of spirituality behind their success. Seeing that we are all human beings on a spiritual experience, this discovery took me on a rather unique approach of pursuing that notion, in doing so also being able to the putting together of this book. During my research into some of the causes of addictions, I discovered what Albert Einstein called the "optical delusion", this is also known by what some may call a form of "myopia" or nearsightedness. This is not to minimize in any way any very real physical/psychological trauma that may have been experienced by other addicts, nor is it intended to be a replacement of medical/ psychological therapy/ advice.

Nearsightedness, is based on ones inability to recognize the dangers as they approach, this myopia continues until they are almost right in front of us. Myopia can and does exist in many areas of our daily activities. This is mainly due to the fact that people all around the world want to live in a perfect world and also "want to believe in magic". They do this as a release from the all too demanding structures we have put in place called reality. This "magical thinking" I now believe to be the main reason behind recreational drug/ substance, use/abuse. Being experimental in nature, and not knowing the real danger(s) associated with various addictions do not spare us from, and lead us to the very real world of addictions.

These feel good chemicals distract the mind, allowing it to not give this myopia the attention it deserves. Addictions caused by a medical condition can and are deserving of the appropriate attention to this "myopia". This myopia can also be associated with an all too well understood condition of "resistance" to a mediation and/or drug. For this you will have to consult your medical/ psychological professional.

Myself being the curious type as to the who(m)/ what is what? In my efforts to get a better understanding of addictions and how to free myself of them I did some research and was unable to get a quality answer from any qualified individual regarding this concept of "God". I decided to look to other sources of information to see what I could discover on my own. Following this course of study has led me into many other areas of interest such as philosophy/ metaphysics/psychology/ biology and even exploring my own spirituality and theology. Having learned these subjects firsthand puts me in the position of being "uniquely qualified" to explain them to you.

Dr. C.G. Jung said "that all psychological theory is also a personal confession", and this is especially true of these areas that speak of the inner figures and personalities of the psyche, such as the shadow/ the anima/us and the self.

During the 31 years spent in the workforce I have learned/ witnessed and experienced a lot of diverse behavior that will be discussed in this book, and this behavior will also help you not only overcome various difficulties but also assist you in achieving the various goals that you have set for yourself? The writing of this book and sharing the information I have found with you in both an enlightening/ entertaining and thought provoking way is another one of my goals. I trust I have.

I have cut grass/ shoveled snow/ swept parking lots/ stained fences/ worked as a carpenter for 15 years/ truck driver for another 12 and even trained as a commercial pilot obtaining my flight instructor rating for fixed wing aircraft. All of these occupations have remained passions of mine even though I have had many other unrelated and sometimes unpaid occupations as I am sure you have as well, just pay those bills.

Every day, many people around the globe are faced with situations and decisions resulting in/from addictions. Contrary to your individualistic way of thinking you are not alone when it comes to dealing with addictions/ other bad habits. We are all a part of the whole. Don't blame yourself that is just your ego getting in the way again.

There is no end to the information that one can learn regarding this subject. The system presented in this book is not that of a closed system, meaning that overtime and as new information is brought forward this system will also become more advanced, and evolve with it. This is the main reason why a user of this system is asked to personalize it to your own specific cases.

I have developed and continue to use this system when dealing with most of the very same issues as you. I have used this system exclusively over the years losing up to 80 lbs. and keeping it off for over two years. I have also used it to quit smoking/ drinking/ drug abuse and even while dealing with some of the mental health issues I have had to face in the past/ present.

As people learn how/ why to set goals as well as the importance of staying with them they will also be able to identify winning strategies of behavior than will inevitably contribute to making their life more productive and enjoyable.

This book has been designed to be used as a pocket reference and motivational guide. Unlike some other programs that require the assistance of professionals, this system requires you to be a self-starter while working at your own pace.

While I was developing this method I was also able to identify a repeating pattern of behavior amongst many different individuals. This behavior patterns is what has become my four step system. These four steps naturally follow each other allowing you to fully understand the process.

I HAVE INTRODUCED THEM TO YOU ON PAGE 67.

Also while developing this method I came up with three words that I used to get me into the basic mindset you need to have. I like to refer to them as the 3'D's. These three words are;

DESIRE/DETERMINATION/DRIVE

Because behavior can be described using various adjectives such as: spontaneous/ automatic/ mechanistic and even ritualistic, I have incorporated in a limited way relevant topics such as biology/ philosophy/ psychology/ metaphysics and yes even theology in order to give you a better picture of the "big you" and why we do some of the things we do. Trying to understand and overcome human behavior can for most be a rather challenging task, nevertheless it can be done.

"The Behavioral System for Weight Loss", my first booklet, was originally copyright in 1989 and again revised in 2007. A more descriptive title could have been "In the Pursuit of Understanding". Because my theory has taken on a life of its own I have decided to publish this new book called "Understanding & Overcoming Addictions" made easy.

Information contained in this system is not mutually exclusive to those in pursuit of a higher education, although that is the end result.

People are always telling me that experience is the best teacher and this is true especially when one exhibits the tendency to think clearly and creatively, both of which are not taught in the educational system. More often than not these same people do not give anyone without this higher education an opportunity to prove themselves. They feel the need to validate their own ego and personal investment in their own education.

I am an internally driven individual, for the most part also self-taught. I have had the opportunity to attend various courses being offered by people with higher education claiming to have degrees, although some did, in the presented subject matter. I was always disappointed with their lack of original material/ philosophy/ theory. We can't all be followers standing on the shoulders of others, just in case they too are

9

wrong. I feel it is sometimes necessary to develop and prove our own theories and methodology.

Instead of allowing ourselves to be manipulated by these emotions we need to learn how to recognize and overcome them learning instead how to be more passionate and happy with ourselves. We can only be passionate about things we care about and excite us. When we decide to take this approach we become more involved in our communities, families and those activities that we participate in. Beginning to understand our communities may lead us to creating a more understanding/ compassionate society, but one must be careful because we can also find the faults and shortcomings of our society. This is a natural tendency because even the word "community" contains the root words "unity" and "common". Here it has been changed for convenience together meaning a common unity.

I also believe that human nature is based on our primordial emotions of fear and anger. Later on I will explain how and why I believe this. Emotions and Feelings are not the same thing. Just like hunger and happiness are not the same, although they are both internal to the individual.

I believe the various subjects that concern themselves with the study of human behavior should be taught in school long before the university level. The problem facing many is the fact that most of us just aren't ready.

If the population was ready and these subjects where taught, then people would be aware of the importance of their decision making process much earlier in life possibly preventing some of them from making the poor choices that they sometimes do. Some of these choices can take the form of addictions, and yes they can also be political. Yes we have on many occasions elected people/ persons to a position they we not equipped to handle or did a poor job at. Then we re-elect them! When people make poor choices it quite often not only reflects on the person and/or society but also becomes a burden on them/it as well.

As mentioned previously "Understanding & Overcoming Addictions" made easy is not just a set of steps to help you lose weight, it can also be used to assist you in the conscious choice of goal setting and your sense of achievement. This sense of achievement can be found only when we have successfully overcome our addictions and/or other bad habits or have achieved a goal that we have set for ourselves. The words accomplishment and achievement here are inter-changeable.

These four steps you will find inescapable when you are "goal oriented".
We have all heard others say that some people can/ will never change. Well that may be true in some cases but it does not have to be true in your case. Past behavior

does not necessarily predict future behavior. People can and do change every day. The secret is in knowing how.

Human nature is what has given us language/ the ability to communicate in great numbers/ organize and to even be competitive. Because people are people and human nature is what it is, we also have ability to be selfishly-ambitious this ability utilizes our inherent character trait known as the "inferiority complex". This is an area of our personality also used in goal setting and its accomplishment. Don't worry because it affects everyone, each in its own way, and each to its own degree. Anything we do or want to accomplish must be firstly selfish, you have got to want to do it, this also incorporates our primordial emotion fear. By wanting to possess that which we do not yet have, will in some way enable us to feel better about ourselves when we are able to possess it.

Fear has existed in our psyche since before our hunter-gatherer days of yester year, when we lived in the cave of shadows. We have come a long way since then but it hasn't been without a lot of personal effort in order to overcome and even understand these primal emotions. By learning to forgive and understand each other as well as learning to work together and being at peace with ourselves is the best we can do.

And then there are those that will inevitably get in our way and present us with challenges we must learn to successfully navigate ourselves around continuing to strive towards our objective (**GOAL**) whatever that may be. We also need to understand human nature and other personality traits to have a more thorough understanding. Applying these lessons learned to potential future situations.

In late 2015 I had finally put this book together, along with two other books I was working on called "decoded" and "spirituality and the human experience". The original manuscript were in digital form contained on a "usb" stick and sub sequentially stolen by whom I considered to be a paid police informant named Ryan Ice Anderson-Sutton. Ryan, or Ryan Anderson for short.

Ryan is an employee of a rather well known multi-national charity operating a shelter/ a half-way house and a soup kitchen. The thrift store they used to operate had to be shut down due to apparent internal mismanagement. They tried to cover this up in an article published in the local newspaper blaming their supporters of giving them all their junk. WOW! what a way to thank your supporters/ customers. This charity is locally known as the "Land of the Black Eyed Jesus" because of the frequency of violent acts of both staff and clients directed towards each other. It is rather absurd; to say the least, that ignorance of the experiences I have to offer should be twisted into an accusation against me. This is what this charity is rather good at as well as playing favorites.

This caused me concern and I felt I had no choice but to question their belief system. They do in fact promote their "soup kitchen" and in doing so encourage others to partake in it. They enjoy boasting that they serve about 200 people lunch and dinner Monday through Friday, with their numbers growing. They I am sure do not know/ care about how this activity affects those (long term) people who utilize the "soup kitchen", after all they themselves have told me that they are in it for the money and for funding dollars numbers matter. It is the nature of this growing dependency, and the negative effect it has/ will have on this/ any community that is cause for alarm.

It seems to me that the people behind the "soup kitchen" have over the past 20 or so years created this need. Just like that of the marketers of "Listerine". Halitosis was not a problem until people were informed that they do not have to put up with it any more. Now there is something we can do about it. These people really had no useful purpose in life so that is why they created the need for the "soup kitchen". I remember working there many years ago when people would and where able to feed and cook for themselves. It must be their way of satisfying their "inferiority complex".

The territorial and federal government is so impressed by their activities, if they only knew; they have largely funded a new building more than 20X its present size. The local first nation's band has also invested a great deal of money into this project.

I believe and am now convinced that in participating willingly in this activity people are learning/ have learned to be "helpless". Learned helplessness is rampant here in Whitehorse. I think a lot of this dependency is because people do not feel good about themselves. It is their way of getting back at the system. Magical thinking if you will, this way of thinking is of course self-defeating because the more they use the system the more money the government throws at it. The only way to beat this system is to avoid it all together. They would feel much better about themselves if they had an affordable and clean place to call their own and where able to avoid it. Housing is that basic need. Many of the people using the soup kitchen do not have a decent place to call home.

Just prior to the stealing of this "usb" stick along with over $1000 in cash, and just over $10,000 in belongings', Ryan had phoned the RCMP on the evening of March 7, 2016, to pick me up and have me incarcerated for a breach of bail charge, because he knew I was out on bail from a drunk driving charge and having alcohol was a violation of one of many bail conditions. He did this even while I was in my own room. I happened to be renting from him at the time. I didn't do anything to bring this on. I was in fact looking for another place to live, I couldn't move out fast enough. If I only knew what was going through his head. I was extremely concerned at the time of this incident that this was a set up for the commission of another crime, and it was the subsequent robbery that did in fact take place and Ryan committed thinking, of course that I wouldn't notice, but even if I did when I do find out, and I did, I couldn't prove it and that he could get away with. Well he was right. I also had a difficult time believing Ryan could/ would stoop so low as to not mind his own business and turn in a friend. I guess I was not a friend just another source of cash after all this was not the first time Ryan did this to a tenant. He apparently had quite the reputation regarding matters such as this. As a result of all this including the impaired driving charge, I was sentenced to a 7 month jail term.

He at the same time as he ratted me out and stole everything from me he was also involved in scamming a young lady out of about $1200 a month rent for a 80 sq.' room also in his trailer and this guy works for the local "Black Eyed Jesus"! Well this young lady, Ryan said in court under oath, was the one who stole much of my belongings. I am still convinced that Ryan had something to do with it. Well this really makes me wonder? What exactly are they teaching them and what is their hiring policy? They seem to be playing their part and seem to be also part of the problem with housing / substance abuse in this community. If you can't trust the "Black Eyed Jesus" who can you trust?

While in custody, at Whitehorse Correctional Center (WCC), I made numerous attempts to safeguard my belongings with no response from either Ryan or his employer, the charity known locally as the "Land of the Black Eyed Jesus". When I inquired further they, the charity known as the "Land of the Black Eyed Jesus" said they could not get involved and returned to me the letter I had written them. They have earned their name. I also, while in custody, asked Ryan if he had a problem with me using his name and the surrounding events in this book to let me know. This book does contain actual events and the names of the guilty have not been changed even though Ryan (Ryan Ice Anderson-Sutton) was given an opportunity to contest this decision as well as ample time to respond. He did not respond or challenge this request. The charity mentioned in this book does exist but I have changed its' name.

Ryan claims to have been jailed for 18 months previously for an arson charge in Edmonton, Alberta some 20 years ago. Mentally I don't think he ever got out, he treats people with undeserved contempt, enjoys arguing doesn't seem to be well liked and appears to be rather creepy and disturbed even in his own trailer.

His behaviors and attitude seem to be consistent with those presently in protective custody (pc) which he admitted he did his time. It wasn't until I was in WCC that these character traits made themselves known. They don't exist in the general population which is where I did my time. I also had a job in the kitchen, where I went from dish washer to the "coffee/ tea/jam and butter" guy.

In my attempt to recover from memory what information was lost regarding this book, I have done my best to put it on paper. After having done so I have added a couple of chapters I only wished could have been on the original, but in hind sight am glad they were not. These couple of chapters must have been of "divine intervention". Although I do not have a formal education in topics discussed doesn't mean I am not knowledgeable and uniquely qualified to discuss them as they appear throughout this book.

I am writing this book from memory and also from my jail cell (located in "G" dorm) located in Whitehorse, Yukon. This facility is known as Whitehorse Correctional Center (WCC). While sitting in my cell I decided to write another letter to the "Black Eyed Jesus" asking them once again for their assistance in this matter. That is recovering my possessions from Ryan Anderson's trailer, and keeping it for me until I can reclaim it from them. Their response was to me they cannot get involved. I thought that was a fitting denial because they were already involved through Ryan. What a cover! Who (m) would a thought?! In a court of law this would be known as collusion/ or even "influence peddling". I wonder why the judge ignored this. Does the "Land of the Black Eyed Jesus" carry that much influence? Or are they to under investigation?

Upon release from WCC, I noticed Ryan outside on the sidewalk immediately adjacent to the "Land of the Black Eyed Jesus "and asked him about my money and belongings, his reply to this was that the money is gone and so are most of my belongings. Well I considered that to be an admission. I said to him "that it was not his to give away" and I want it back. His reply to that was "take me to court", so I did just that. We eventually did go to court and the presiding judge decided to rule in favor of Ryan (the informant) claiming that I abandoned my belongings. To me this was not a surprise, more of a confirmation of the "bias", and even "collusion" of the charity Ryan works for. I did not however, abandon my belongings as the judge decided; he just did not accept my evidence. I was able to however to recover 2/3 of my belongings and an order for Ryan to return the stolen money. Even that I had to get a garnishee for. And this is all after he admitted it on court documents. After all is said and done this process still took 1 1/2 years.

All this happened before I was informed by two separate legal professionals that Ryan Anderson is in fact a paid police informant. This incident also happened within 2 days of Ryan receiving my months' rent of $800, which the month before was only $700 because I paid cash and social assistance was not involved. I later learned from the "Yukon Human Rights Commission" they consider it to be discrimination towards an individual when rent is set solely based on their source of income in this case and many others it is social assistance .As you can see the writing of this book has had its ups and down as well as its unique set of setbacks, and is a culmination of events taken place in Whitehorse, Yukon Canada, however, that does not make it geographically exclusive, I am sure you will find parallels in your community as well.

There is an apparent shortage of affordable housing and /or descent accommodation in Whitehorse, Yukon and trying to find affordable housing is very difficult. I am currently living in an overpriced motel room, yes this too is a "Yukon Human

Rights" issue. This situation is also not geographically exclusive; however it does seem to be systemic, and by this I mean it has been noticeable and growing for the past 20 years. When I arrived back to Whitehorse, after living in Ontario for the past 18 years, I lived in my car for the first month.   I then found a room in a run-down basement of a very old three storied wood frame walkup. I was there for six months and couldn't wait to move out. Ryan offered me a room in his trailer for a little more money and Ryan was just as guilty as the many others when it came to overcharging tenants rent strictly based upon their source of income. Although I thought it wasn't legal I did not know for sure until it was much too late to do anything about it.

I met Ryan while I was working at the local "Black Eyed Jesus". I had a job working as a residential support worker at the "Black Eyed Jesus" which is fancy way to say I worked at the shelter. Ryan was/ is the janitor there and has been for several years, or so he says. I always thought there was something odd about Ryan. I guess it was a combination of his lack of teeth/ tall/ goofy looking with a stutter. His standoffish body language should've clued me in to a psychopathic personality. Ryan Anderson is white about 140 lbs. crew cut sandy brown hair/ no teeth/ stammers and is about 5"-10" tall. He seems to enjoy smoking crack/marijuana and betting on sporting events/ he also seems to enjoy   taking advantage of the clients at his place of employment by selling cigarettes (which is against the policy) and bad mouthing people whether he knows them or not, and then there is the impulse control, or lack thereof. He seems to enjoy stammering and mimicking people when it is in his best interest, this is how he plays on your feelings getting that sympathy vote.

While I was working at the local "Black Eyed Jesus" I was informed as to how to deal with various individuals that came in "under the influence" of either drugs or alcohol. We were told to write them up on reports and put their name on the "shit list". Well to be quite honest with you I thought the clients to be real people going through some of life's difficulties. The real culprits were the staff at the "Black Eyed Jesus "they seem to be vindictive/ back biters and I thought their names should be included on the "shit list". This charities name seems to be fitting as far as the staff is concerned.

After having arrived back in Whitehorse after living in Ontario over the past 18 years, I noticed that the soup kitchen had really gone downhill since I left in 1997. I think it went under another name. I used to work there but can't remember now. It was almost "unrecognizable". So much so that I felt like the Spirit had also left and what appeared to be the walking dead took over. It was like the tail wagging the dog or maybe a "mutiny"!

One day, after having seen one of the many employees of the "Black Eyed Jesus" repeatedly violating this charities policy by not only coming to the workplace while off duty as many did. They arrived in an intoxicated state. After a couple of weeks of deliberating about this I decided I too have had enough of their mocking/ dis- respect/ dis-regard for the needs of their clients along with the poor example they were portraying as well as their self-righteous attitude. So in a drunken stupor and off duty I to figured I would also give them a taste of their own medicine, so I proceeded through the door into the shelter/ through what they the dining hall, and walked straight to the kitchen area erased the clients names off the "shit-list" and put "BLACK EYED JESUS STAFF C-GOD". I guess the management didn't appreciate it and suspended me for 7 months, oh well I am better off without them.

The attitude in there had gotten so bad and the atmosphere had also gotten so toxic over the previous years that even the two pictures of Jesus had black eyes. I assume this is how they earned the name and reputation of the land of the "Black Eyed Jesus'. It was these events that eventually landed me in WCC and my original manuscript stolen. You might think that they were trying to cover up something? I have heard of the "One Eyed Jack" but never until now the "Black Eyed Jesus"!

As we will learn actions and body language speak louder than words. These two combined make up to 80% of communication. Their denial is actually an admission. They can't see it nor can they do the right thing! Until they learn to step back and look at themselves they will be doomed to repeat it over and over again. They have now been operating like this for about 18 years. Apparently this started shortly after I left in 1997 and the "officers" shortly thereafter, with poor quality leadership/ guidance only to follow. They remind me about the story of Ali Babba and the 40 thieves.

This book also happens to be the study of human behavior that has kept me occupied for many years. Why do we do the things we do? It is that question that has led me into fields of study such as biology/ psychology/ metaphysics/ philosophy/ theology and many others, as well as various addictions that I have experienced and have successfully overcome.

As stated earlier the information contained in this book is not exclusively limited to those engaged in the institutes of higher learning, although we do become just that, wiser and more in tune (intuitive) with what we have learned and remembered through discussion/ observation and even participation. We gain a deeper understanding about who we are as individuals the "Big You" and how we interact with the outside world and vice versa.

I believe the problem with the housing issue here begins about 20 years ago with the intentional closing of a hotel known as "The Fourth Avenue Residence". The "Fourth Avenue Residence" was closed as a low-cost housing solution, renovated and turned into a pricey hotel called "The High Country Inn" now called the "Coast Inn".   The "Fourth Avenue Residence" was a convenient/ low cost/ clean/ friendly place for people to stay either by the week/ month/ day.

When it was closed the people, and there where many, were forced to find accommodations, many being unsuitable or not available. Problems facing the people of Whitehorse are not new they are systemic. The people know there is a problem but they cannot identify it nor would they know how to fix it. What they do is build band aid solutions such as drug and rehabilitation centers and modernize their correctional facility. This will not fix the problem.

I know that the problem is a psychological one and that is affordable housing!

I hope you enjoy the rest of this book as much as I did in putting it all together for you.

TABLE OF CONTENTS

FOOD ENERGY

FOOD IS, a basic human need according to Psychologist Abraham Maslow who was able to identify this and wrote about its' importance in his theory of the "Hierarchy of needs" or as some may call it his "Hierarchy of Motivations".

Food energy comes in a form we call calories. Calories and nutrients come in the form of food. There are 3500 calories in a pound. Our bodies require these calories in order to convert them into energy in order to nourish our bodies and also assist it in performing the various functions that it does. These functions can be either unconscious biological/ psychological, or conscious physical activities we participate in. Excess calories are converted into fat and stored in various areas within our body.

When you are shopping for food also called groceries, try and avoid those impulse buys.
Impulse buys can account for up to a 20% increase in spending and also in food waste on a personal level. It has been observed that corporations can have up to 30% food waste. Grocery stores have in the past enlisted the support of behavioural psychologists in order to keep customers, in their store longer while spending more money. Impulse buys are generally low price and will attract your attention immediately. Using various colour schemes is another way psychologists

have lured customers into various parts of the store. I can't remember the last time I went to the store for only 1 item, only to return with 4 or5.

Manufactures' as well as growers have lobbied the government over the past several decades to include products into their food even though there presence is not in the customers best interest nutritionally speaking. These four foods are; sugar/ salt/ fat and yes even corn. Even though these four ingredients seem to be ubiquitous, and trying to avoid them completely is unrealistic, you will find it beneficial to avoid them whenever possible. You can do this by checking your labels and keeping them to a minimum.

SUGAR/SALT/FAT/CORN

FOOD ENERGY IS MEASURED IN UNITS CALLED CALORIES

1 GRAM OF PROTEIN= 4 CALORIES
100 GRAMS SUGAR= 387 CALORIES
1 GRAM CARBOHYDRATE= 4 CALORIES
1 GRAM FAT= 9 CALORIES
100 GRAMS ALCOHOL= MORE THAN 200 CALORIES
1 POUND= 3500 CALORIES
OUR BODIES ARE CONSIST OF ABOUT 80% WATER, AND WATER WEIGHS IN AT 10 POUNDS PER GALLON (4.54L)

EMPTY CALORIES SUCH AS THOSE FOUND IN ALCOHOL AND JUNK FOOD HAVE NO NUTRITIONAL VALUE WHATSOEVER.
A BODY AT REST REQUIRES ABOUT 100 CALORIES PER HOUR JUST TO MAINTAIN BIOLOGICAL FUNCTIONS SUCH AS BREATHING AND HEART RATE.

Salt will enable you to retain water which is not always a good idea. Sugar on the other hand will over time harden your arteries and lead to heart disease. Both salt and sugar will lead to high blood pressure. Because an increase in body weight can also be the result of weight training I feel I should also inform you that muscle weighs twice as much as fat and of course is much healthier for you. Corn seems to be used as filler as well as an additive such as corn syrup, corn starch.

Alcohol can be an addictive substance. When we consume those empty calories such as those found in alcohol and that other food group called "junk food "the weight we gain is the result of our body converting those calories into a form of sugar known as glucose then storing it as fat. It seems to me the more weight we gain the more alcohol we require to achieve the same level. These empty calories gained do us no favours. They are just along for the ride, slowing us down as a result, making us feel heavier and realizing that "gravity" is not always your friend.

In order for a person to lose 1 pound of body weight they would have to reduce their caloric intake by 3500 calories., Right? Point to remember is that when you lose weight the first 10 pounds is water. This is because our bodies are 80% water. After the water weight has gone there may be a period where you notice no reduction even though you have reduced your caloric intake. This is common and is referred to as a plateau. These plateaus are a part of the cycle. Your body also has to constantly read adjust itself. Many people get discouraged at this point, you will need to remain on the calorie reduced program and stay focused on the end result of achieving your **GOAL.**

When you consume less than required amount of calories your body will then have to make up the difference. It does this by breaking down the fat molecules/ converting them into sugar so that it can be used as fuel for the body. This process is known as "ketosis". If you overdue it then you run the risk of your body also converting muscle and bone mass into sugar for fuel. This will inevitably lead to more complicated medical procedures or even damage to your muscular/ skeletal systems such as premature atrophy or osteoporosis. Carbonated water such as those found in soft drinks have been associated with osteoporosis.

Carbohydrates are also a type of sugar known as glucose. Our bodies convert this glucose to be stored as fat that may be converted into energy at some later date. Root vegetables contain a vast amount of glucose (sugar) and are classified as carbohydrates. Trying to obtain more energy than required will obviously result in our bodies storing this excess as fat.

We tend to overeat when we are either really hungry or stressed. It takes time for your enzymes to tell your brain you are full. Many of us eat until we feel full by this time it is too late.

People have been known to eat for a variety of reasons. For example anticipation/ smell/ taste/ texture/noise/ sport/ hunger/ suggestion/ impulse/ nourishment/ unconscious/ testing/guilt/ snacking/ boredom/ joy of elimination from either or both ends or would that be anticipation? Then there are those that get paid to eat! You know those "motivational eaters"!

Which one(s) are you? It has been said that cancer cells cannot live in an acidic environment. are you "toxic"?

Smell is a very strong motivator, triggering impulsive/ irrational behavior such as eating, drinking, and smoking. Smell also, because it is associated with our feeling of anticipation, releases a brain chemical known as dopamine. This is because we have, over time linked these smells (aromas) to our behavior that gives us pleasure. This is our feel good chemical. Why is dope called dope? This dopamine also induces pleasure and relaxation. Evidence of this can be found in the success of those involved in the aroma therapy industry.

Smell is also connected with our ability to taste food. Food that smells good probably also tastes good and may also be good for you also. If you have a cold you probably can't even taste your food. Smoking also affects our ability to taste food. This could be because of the heat of the smoke we are inhaling and have done damage to our taste buds.

EMOTIONS

UNDERSTANDING our emotions is important because we all have them and are frequently influenced by those of other people. We also need to learn the difference between feelings and emotions, they are not the same, however they can be closely related with only a thin line betwixt them. It is beyond the scope of this book to explain them in detail. If they are that important to you then please refer to your medical/ psychological practitioner.

Dr. Sigmund Freud's view was that "Human Beings" are born at odds with our environment. We are wired in a way Freud and his contemporaries understood animals to be. We must be oriented towards pursuing simple pleasures with reckless/ ruthless abandonment.

It is our unique ability to not only learns in a non-instinctual manner but to teach these new found approaches to "others". These approaches enable us correct what we find as a collective unacceptable, and to encourage behaviours that we do find acceptable. This allows us to build faith and trust in "others". In building these feelings in "others" enables us to live in what we call "communities". This allows our communities to also develop and take on a life of their own, eventually turning into what we call "cities". A community was always meant to be more than just a collection of individuals pursuing their own objectives with no common interest and not in pursuit of the common good.

We are all born innocent yet demanding/ not knowing right/wrong/good/evil. If we were all born inherently evil I believe there would be no hope, therefore we must be born inherently good, having been equipped with the proper equipment and basic emotion needs such as the capability to express;

LOVE/HAPPINESS/FEAR/ANGER

It is the primitive part of our personality called the "id" that is at play here. Because the "id "is impulsive and needs to know it exists it requires us to be demanding attention. Without the ability to use language our "id" urges us to use sound(s) to communicate. Even the animals have this ability.

The vast majority of our emotions stem from one of the four mentioned above. For example the emotion of greed originates in our primal emotion fear as does jealousy. Wrath is an emotion following that of rage which is not the same as fear but is more complex. Anger is another emotion that can influence our feelings. Anger has also been called righteous. The difference between the two is righteous anger has the majority of people benefitting from it whereas in the original it is to the benefit of the person portraying it.

FEAR/ANGER/HATE/RAGE/WRATH

Even human nature is inherently selfish and of course it too is built upon fear and anger and our inherent "inferiority complex". Our very nature is to defy both death and pain. If you think about this for a moment then you will also realize that it is fear that is the opposite of love. A person cannot hate what they first do not fear. The Christian bible tells us in 108 places to fear not. You might then ask yourself what is fear based on and the answer would have to be the "unknown" or "other". We fear what we do not understand and where there is" other", there is also fear.

People are primarily afraid of change because with change comes both the "other" and the "unknown". Change can also be good and necessary.

Fear is our most primitive emotion which is why so many others are associated with it.
Dr. C.G. Jung said "We are guided by our fates, by those archetypal powers far beyond our conscious will and/or knowledge. Also the absence of the anima/us in our psychological life is the nature of depression.

As human beings we all have an underlying "inferiority complex" and if I asked you what are you afraid of? What would you say? Many people are afraid of pain or discomfort, such as what is experienced when one decides to overcome a bad habit or addiction. These are the effects of withdrawal.

We all seem to be afraid of something! This is where this book seems to be most effective and why it is suggested that you carry it with you as a reference guide.

Fear comes in two forms. There is the rational and then there is the irrational. The irrational fear is the imagined product of the magical mind. These fears are like shadows/noises and even rumour. Things that present us with no real danger. This type of fear could've been the original type. When we lived in the cave of shadows not knowing real fear is when you leave the cave and get eaten by a tiger. That is rational fear. We fear what we do not understand. Fear is a learned behaviour. Fear is the emotion we use to solve this unknown. The fear of God is the beginning of wisdom. Fear the one who cannot only kill the body but cast your soul into hell. The gift of fear is intuition. Fear also helps in making us think quickly and clearly as a stimulant. Fear and anger equals aggression. Learn to use aggression, aggression breeds aggression, aggression turned inwards equals resolve and determination/ aggression turned outward equals violence/ inappropriate behavior. Panic leads to confusion. Anger also helps us to pursue the more difficult unknown.

Unfortunately we are all afraid of something it is in our biological makeup. Without fear we may not have survived the cave of shadows. We are a predator species with binocular vision and eyes on the front of our head. We are also a brave species by learning what is around the evolutionary corner. Fear seems to work in our benefit and is for now at least the catalyst that seems to make things happen. Without fear we might become complacent and nothing would get done. We would then suffer from excessive boredom having no motivation to get anything done.

You are probably wondering how we overcome fear. You must first understand that fear is based on both the "unknown" and the "other". In order to conquer both, one needs to use knowledge. Just as light dispels darkness, knowledge dispels the fear contained in both the "other" and the "unknown"

I am sure you are familiar with the saying that we fear what we do not understand, and where there is "other" there is fear. While trying to answer that question myself I have had to dig through various books on philosophy and psychology. I seemed to have a "eureka" moment when I realized that when we prejudge people or situations this leads us to the "other" and the "unknown". Because we want to know more about this, these questions seem to create the very mystery we are trying to solve. We must be careful not to let anger enter the situation because anger brings with it frustration and this can only cloud our decision making process and yes, perhaps our better judgement as well.

While studying Zen Buddhism I learned the importance of not pre-judging situations or people but to accept them as they unfold. The gift of fear is intuition we must also learn to use this wisely. The German language has a word that describes this. It is "Geshenlassen" meaning let it happen.

Trying to overcome fear is one thing and completely overcoming it is possible using more evolved emotions such as forgiveness/understanding/love/happiness. If we hope to understand ourselves on a deeper level then we must put our best effort forward. During my studies in Zen I had another "eureka" moment when I was contemplating the yin/yang symbol. This symbol if you are not aware depicts the struggle betwixt the two Omni-present forces in this world, and they are good/evil. These forces are present in the spiritual realm as well as in nature. My "eureka" moment came when I realized that because evil is based on fear/ anger it can only exist when it has something to feed upon. By learning to overcome fear using more complex emotions such as compassion/love/happiness we deny it something to feed upon. Therefore in conclusion because fear/ anger are self-defeating it will feed upon itself eventually destroy itself. The portion representing the love/ happiness portion will as its design and nature will expand and overcome.

Love is humankinds' most complex/ highest emotion and because of this it is also a standalone emotion. This emotion is designed to be given away. The more you give it away the more you will receive and this too must be given away. Many religions and philosophies around the world perpetuate the same message regarding this emotion. Love thy neighbour/ do unto others as you would have them do unto you/ faith/ hope/ love. There is much more to say regarding this emotion.

God is love…. . Love is…, it is not ours to keep. Love is a positive emotion supporting happiness and goodness. Just as its opposite fear supports anger and evil. Faith/ hope/ love the greatest of these is love. Why? Some people consider apologizing and showing respect a weakness when in actual fact it is strength of character and purpose. If we lived in a world where Love was in charge, then perhaps we would all become complacent and nothing would get done. Learned helplessness would be everywhere and we would once again be living in the cave of shadows, afraid of that tiger that will eat you. Humankind's collective ego would not allow this to happen. Therefore, what I said earlier about the need to understand human nature and the learning in order to overcome fear also has to exist.

Fear of God is the beginning of wisdom. What is wisdom? Well I believe wisdom to be the correct and/or proper use of knowledge. Where do we get this knowledge? We get it through discussion/ reading/

communication techniques and even body language which is non-verbal yet very effective. If we can also use knowledge to overcome fear then we can also learn that God is love. I believe this might help explain why love is humankinds most powerful and complex emotion. For in the Christian bible in the book of Genesis is said that after Adam ate what Eve had offered him the serpent said "now they will be like us knowing good from evil". It can only be through the pursuit of this knowledge that we are able to make sense of this experience.

I believe that many of the super-rich people around the world who claim that they would give it all away just aren't able to give it away fast enough. This is probably due to the vast amount of interest they receive/ received/ will receive, also in part to "divine intervention". The super-rich are not able to wash their hands of their apparent "Greed". One does not have to look too far to see the effects of this greed. Greed also seems to be based on fear. The economic collapse of 2008 is a good example of this. What are they afraid of? Or who (m) are they angry with? Is this how they deal with their "inferiority complex"? Is this how you will deal with yours and does this help or hinder your personal growth and progress? I believe because of the shattering of the worlds' economy in 2008, as of 2016 I also believe the worlds' economy still has not recovered. I know mine hasn't!

Some people will at times find themselves in a state of "desperation" for one thing or another. If this should happen to you, you need to pay attention to this because of the feeling it invokes. The feeling of desperation can be also associated with anger/fear/panic and can also be irrational. Desperation can also lead a person to be hyper-competitive leading to a sociopathic/ psychopathic behaviour. This is a dangerous place to be emotionally because of its ability to rob one of compassion and conscience. Evidence of this can be found in places where the economics support employers offering employees part time work with minimum wage opportunities also in dead end jobs with "glass ceilings". People experiencing this are noticeably unhappy and always seem to be in a hurry going from A-B-C-D-E... .

A person does not have to be a criminal to be a sociopath/ psychopath. A sociopath/ psychopath doesn't even need to be human. Corporations in law have "person status" but are not human, yet they are able to exhibit humanlike qualities such as sociopathy/psychopathy as well as exhibiting hyper-competitive behaviour.

Sociopathic/ psychopathic behaviour is one of many character traits that can be found in any walk of life. Even computers have the tendency to be either a sociopath or a psychopath! They never forget a thing and will even try to outthink you. They can even be the world's biggest tattle tales, and even keep secrets from you! We even have to compete against a computer whether it be a robot or not for various employment opportunities. These employment opportunities are growing everyday more and more in their favour.

Human nature is based on the unknown and sometimes our emotions boil over. We have many different emotions and it is beyond the scope of this book to describe them all. Therefore I will stick to the ones I consider the big players in our daily struggle to overcome addictions and/or in our dealing effectively with them.

When it comes to the rich versus the poor, well the poor reminds the rich that they too are still mortal, sickness or in health/ richer or poorer till death do we part. We cannot as of yet transcend to the immortal without first passing through death. An important point to remember is that whether a person is considered to be poor or in poverty it remains a state of mind. Many people fall into this category yet do not let the situation get them down. They seemed to have risen above life's;' circumstances.
One's true self- Dkayaharma. Mortality is but an illusion. We have invented these boundaries that enslave us. On day we will all wake up!

On the psychological side abolish the repressive approach as they have done with toilet training/

punishments/ and other traumatic experiences and
teach love/ kindness/faith/hope.

Inspiration takes root in the conscious mind.

Eventually, meaning over centuries, we were/are able
to separate ourselves from "mother nature" and
"mother earth" by first stepping out of the cave of
shadows and into the light of knowledge.
When we discovered agriculture we also discovered our
separate self and with it "separation anxiety".
To deal successfully with this "separation anxiety" they
had to convince others that they were safe. This was
their "coping mechanism". This must have taken
centuries because no known language existed, only a
handful of guttural sounds and perhaps body language.
Something had to be fashioned to prove to the observer
that something beneficial could be predicted/ expected.
The best example I can think of is the famous creation
of the "druids" in England known as "Stonehenge".
Without language one can observe/ learn and predict
moon cycles/ seasons also when it is time to plant and
harvest. We will never be completely separate from
"mother earth" or "mother nature" due to obvious
reasons, however it is because of this relationship that
modern day psychology still agrees that "other" in our
life. Is that of our biological mothers and they are the
most important.

We are spiritual beings on a human experience and understanding this experience means we should also understand our biology. In short we are a predator species with our eyes (two of them) conveniently located at the front of our head and binocular vision. We have advanced so far that we can now also correct this binocular vision with the use of corrective lenses.

Technology is also becoming more advanced and is now in direct competition with us for employment across all fields. This result will be an ever increasing unemployment rate with inevitably increasing health and social costs and concerns. This scenario begs us to ask questions regarding the future of humankind. Are we becoming or have we always been a kept species? Or are we a slave species that has been planted here on Earth, learning to think outside the box but have not yet learned our place in the universe. Has this been foretold by the ancient prophets and also in the bibles book of revelation and reveled to us through the Holy Spirit. Has the human race fallen asleep and become reckless in our pursuits. The Canadian government has said in two interviews that by the year 2025, 50% of the work will be gone. This is to say that technology will be capable of doing a better job that "Joe Public". The Canadian government also would not or could not answer the question "what then"? When I pressed them on two occasions regarding this.

It has been said that humankind is now living in what is now known as the age of "Aquarius". It has been said this is the age when humankind will start to think for themselves. I am sure technology has a lot to do with this phenomenon, but I can't help thinking that this was also told to us by the ancient prophets. John of Patmos comes to mind with the "book of Revelation". For those of you who are not in the know this is the last book of the "Holy Bible" In it is said that "God" will pour out his spirit upon all flesh. As a result of this combination it has led to mental health issues such as the ever increasing number of people suffering from various mental health issues that are too numerous to mention here.

I once had a eureka moment while I was studying the yin/yang symbol. This symbol I believe symbolizes the struggle between the two forces present on this planet we call earth. These two forces I believe to be good vs. evil. This is a spiritual battle that in many ways effects the way we think and behave. Some might even go as far as saying that this battle represents the very nature of life itself, survival. This "survival" could just be the evolution of our species into the age of "Aquarius", a coming of age, if you will. These forces exist in the spiritual realm and is the invisible battle between good and evil. Invisible here does not mean unseen, again if you have the eyes to see and the ears to hear. There is another Buddhist saying that also goes something like "learn to listen to that which makes no sound".

Evil is what happens when fear is feeding on anger, and in this example it is feeding upon itself and will ultimately consume itself. Whereas the portion representing the good will ever expand increasing in size because that to is its nature. Therefore evil cannot overpower and rule goodness. There is a Buddhist saying that goes something like "We are all born ready to succeed, we must learn how to fail and endure in order to overcome our own shortcomings, and there can be many for some of us, and in doing so we learn to understand the bigger picture. That is our place in the universe. This can also be useful in our daily struggle in dealing with various addictions issues we face.

I now believe it is not only valid but helps to shape our personality. As we mature we have inevitably spent considerable time around older people. We also absorb the qualities we desire both in speech and behavior. Verbal and non-verbal body language. By incorporating these qualities we open ourselves up to have more of this transformation revealed to us.

If we have the ears to hear and the eyes to see. As we also gain insight into behavior and learning our place in the universe, we also reciprocate this to those around us. Many people will not agree or understand this level of knowledge. There are those of us who become so possessive of this this knowledge that they actually build myths around it in order to deceive others so that they become lost in their endeavor. God freely gives therefore we to should give freely. The bible as we know it is full of wisdom that should be shared amongst other like-minded people. As we grow wise through the use of psychology/ philosophy/religion and even biology we should dig further in the faith, helping us to further understand.

False prophets and evil spirits also pursue this wisdom and also build myths and use fear to discourage others from seeking the truth. It is better to give than to receive, the Christian bible tells us. EX 20-17 tells us not to covet anything that belongs to your neighbor and EX 20-15 tells also not to steal. Some people do not listen and covet that which does not belong to them and then there are those that will go so far as to steal that which does not belong to them. This can and does go as far as their potential apotheosis. The ultimate PRRE or gift cannot be stolen it is an internal quality, bestowed upon the few by God.

People who do not understand quite literally drive themselves "mad" in an attempt to possess that which they do not have. All humankind possesses this potential we just have to awaken to it. There must be in keeping with my theory and internal dialogue initiated by either an external or internal que in order for this seed of inspiration to take root in the conscious mind.

My theory goes as follows;

HEAR
SPEAK
FEEL
BELIEF SYSTEM
EMOTION
ATTITUDE
BEHAVIOUR

For those of us who understand, know that it is a lifelong commitment, one that we cannot break even if we wanted to because we did not choose it, it chose us. The Christian bible states that "it is by their fruits that you will know them". There are those who have fallen asleep and others that do not seem to care.

I believe Jesus Christ was a great prophet that did many great works and because there are many faiths in this world that also recognize him and his wondrous works. The divinity of Jesus Christ is not that of the early Christian movement nor that of the divine God nor is the question of his divinity quintessential to the faith. It is worth noting that only the Christian faith sees Jesus Christ as divine. The apotheosis of man is a very interesting phenomenon and is a kin to the human potential. It is a quality bestowed upon various individuals chosen only by God and certainly not by man. aka "the pope".

When Jesus said "I am the way/ truth and the life no man comes to the father but by me", he had to say this because up until then we (humankind) did not know that we to had the potential. He also said in Luke "the kingdom of God is within you". In psychology they have a term for this belief system and that is either a "God complex" or is a "Megalomaniac". This definition cannot apply to Jesus , although some may think it does, simply because he is/ was as far as we can understand the original "archetype"   the rest of us are just trying to emulate his work. That is ok because it is not a bad thing, it is just another stigma/label we as human beings like to place on each other. We are our own "archetype".

Positive emotions such as love/ happiness are easy to give away and to show. Negative emotions such as anger/ anxiety and fear are more difficult and are usually projected onto its' victim unwittingly and therefore not appreciated. Positive emotions such as love/ happiness/are easy to give away and receive. Smiles are contagious. Try it.

Jealousy can be linked to fear/ our inherent inferiority complex, as well as the power of suggestion. This is an irrational response requiring more extensive though and perhaps meditation.

Perhaps the purpose of nature is first and foremost sustainable, secondly entertainment and to gather and gain insight into the nature of GOD, thirdly to learn how

to co-exist within it. Seeing that the self and others are one, we are released from the fear of life. Seeing that being and non-being are one we are delivered from the fear of death.
For out of nothingness came something and it returned to nothingness.

Over time the amount of individuals who have awakened to the pursuit of enlightenment has always been small (few) and most probably will continue this way for quite some time, until humankind evolves into the realm of the super-consciousness. Except for those few who individually choose the path of enlightenment, it is quite true that history is and will remain the chronicle of men and women born too soon.

Anger can also be expressed as righteous anger. This type of anger is expressed for the greater good as opposed to the will of the aggressor. A good example of this is when Jesus was in the temple when it was being used by merchants to buy and sell. Jesus then overturned the tables and called them all a den of thieves.

MOTIVATORS

ACHEIVEMENT
RECOGNITION
OPPORTUNITY
ADVANCEMENT
RESPONSIBILITY

These motivators make up a continuum ranging from;

NO SATISFACTION--------------------SATISFACTION

ACHEIVEMENT: When you accomplish a goal set by either you or someone else.
RECOGNITION: Getting that well deserved pat on the back for a job well done and/ or appreciation.
OPPORTUNITY: When you are able to give assistance/ direction in the way a person should go or a job be done correctly.
ADVANCEMENT: The act of getting closer to your goal or objective.
RESPONSIBILITY: Having the ability to accept the repercussions of your actions whether they are good or bad.

You also need to believe in yourself. Having faith in yourself and portraying a good attitude seems to go a long way and has a lot to do with those things we choose to do with our life. When you believe in yourself your whole attitude changes and people will also begin to see you and treat you in a manner you feel you are deserving of. Believe it or not this also includes the clothes you wear on any given day. Those things we enjoy we tend to do well at just as those things we do not like we do not do well at.

MEDITATION

WHERE DO you live? For most of us it is not just a physical address it is also a state of mind. Meditation does require practise and is an activity I practise daily, and have for many years now. I do this to not only clear my mind but to also focus on what it is I need to do on a daily/weekly/monthly basis.

Meditation allows me to practise it whenever I feel the need, it keeps me centered in reality allows me to be more productive and it even takes me to my "happy place". Meditation can be thought of accessing and developing that part of our personality known as the "ego". Some have even been known to have reached a state of "nirvana" and "enlightenment through the practise of meditation. In order to do this effectively in the beginning stages you should disconnect from technology if you can or turn it off and remove any other potential distractions.

You must then relax/ clear your mind/ close your eyes/ slow your breathing and heart rate. This will allow you to clear your mind of all the minutia that has accumulated and other thoughts that are not conducive to your mental health. Students actively engaged in the learning curve can really benefit from this technique. Both learning information and retaining it becomes much easier. After this step focus becomes much easier and quicker.

Meditation takes a lifetime to master but if we all practise it then we can all be a work in progress. No one is perfect and by doing this we discover that our growth is in the journey not the destination. We can accomplish much more when our minds are relaxed and focused on what it is we need to do.

Many of us have participated in activities that at first looked interesting and the more we learn about it the less interesting they become, this is normal just keep on looking until you find something that really interests you.

Our personalities are a lot like that as we move forward through life. Not really knowing who we are and why we make the decisions we do. We all need to step back and take a look at ourselves this also happens to be a Buddhist view. We are not only unique but we are also part of the whole and could play a bigger role if only we knew how. For example look at the word "community" in it there is the word "unity", togetherness sharing a common interest. It is a part of our personality called the ego that tells us that we are unique/ separate and detached from others therefore our problems are also unique. We are an individual but our problems are not. When you think of it we all share in personality traits and experiences therefore we must conclude that we are all a part of the whole human race whether we like it or not. We have all come from the same source. Jesus also mentioned this fact when he explained that there are many parts to the body and all are equally important/ also in explaining the parable about the vine and the branches.

A personality profile is a good way/ the only way to get to know the whole you/ the bigger you/the hidden self. Our personality is with us for life and we should only have one. If by chance you do have more than one then you need to see a medical/ psychological professional.

We do not give it much thought, but we all have a shadow personality. For lack of a more descriptive and medically correct word I will use the term "alter ego". This "alter ego" can be either a good thing or a not so good thing, either way we generally keep this to ourselves and don't generally share this with others. As we move forward through life we actually grow into our personality, it is usually not fully developed until perhaps our late 20's early 30's.

It is rather enlightening to realize how important our past is and how it has influenced the person we have become. By learning this life experience can help us avoid any/all pitfalls that may be lying in wait for us in the future through recognition and avoidance. We can also learn to position ourselves to benefit from those decisions we have made.

This process is ongoing and can only end in the death of the physical "self" our spiritual "self" will continue evolving even into the next realm.

When God created us in his image he also gave us what we know as a brain. Along with this came the profound ability to think/ organize in great numbers/ reason/ plan all this independently. We aren't waiting for God, God is waiting for us. God is patient/ kind not wanting any of us to perish but have everlasting life. God wants us to learn how to explore his truth and wonders. He wants us to be more like god like.

This phenomenon known as "apotheosis" has been achieved in the past and therefore can be done again. We the humankind is the problem. We are slow to understand, slow to believe. We have been deceived by the dark side of human nature and feel ashamed and embarrassed and foolish. Our pride has been diminished and even though we know we can and should trust the light are skeptical because we don't fully understand it. Why should we, we haven't lived in the light. This light we thought we lived in has now just been revealed as artificial. Meditate on this and see what you can discover.

When meditating eliminate if possible any "white noise" and if possible create for yourself an area of sensory deprivation. This will assist you with eliminating that "white noise" and minutia caused by unnecessary thoughts. Do you not know that we hear more clearly when our eyes are closed Why? This procedure also helps to eliminate "brain radiation" and/or "thought emissions".

Meditation is used to bring the mind/ body and spirit together. One could say that we use meditation to practice our spirituality. In a world that has become busier with work/ hobbies/ commerce and distractions of all sorts it is not east to find the time, but the time has always been there. Our thinking and corresponding behavior is what has been standing in our way. We do have to learn how to get out of our own way. We also must learn how to be a better, more efficient manager of our time. Because meditation is a rather passive activity we can't just jump in without direction. We need to recognize that meditation is a learned behavior. Some might even say it is "mechanistic" or "ritualistic", but what is wrong with that?

Our mind is our most powerful tool, so why not learn to use it for our benefit instead of not using it to our destruction. Learning to clear our mind of negative thought/ noise and other distractions does take practice and focus.

Conflicting thoughts occur between the ego/id/superego because as Freud put it an infantile allegiance to infantile magic and the mature aspects of our personality are fighting this allegiance. Other may say that this conflict is a form of psychosis.

Neurosis on the other hand is thought od as being a compromise between the id and ego, a damned if I do and a damned if I don't situation. It seems that our super-ego is as some would say lies "just under the surface" and it doesn't take much to surface. Giving in to our addictions makes this behaviour more apparent and even observable so that when trying to overcome them we can see a part of our self in them. This can be considered to be "death of the self' but only part of it. I know this can be difficult for some, but in order to overcome an addiction it is necessary for us to learn the importance of letting this part of our self go, even though I love myself and I am sure that you love yourself. Not all of our self is productive some of our self tends to hinder our progress through this world. We need to evolve as humans, and to evolve means to change. Try not to let your inferiority complex get in the way.

Meditation is used as a tool to help us focus our mind and can be more effective than actual physical effort.

Students can really benefit from meditation. Clearing your mind from minutia allows your brain to relax and catalog important information. This allows your memory to become more vivid and spontaneous. We all enjoy a quick and accurate answer. You can really noticed the difference when a person finds it necessary to cram for an exam, for example. By putting too much information into the brain does not allow you the time needed to adsorb this information. This results in lower scores and shorter than normal memory.

Meditating frequently allows you to access your long term memory making the memory process much easier/ quicker and you should notice better results as well. Why learn the same information 2-3X when you can remember it once. Learn to relax and let your brain do what it was designed to do. The more often we are able to relax our mind the easier it becomes to adsorb and retain this new information. I use the word "ADSORB" instead of Absorb. With added knowledge now forming part of our memory and memory being an integral part of our brain function, when something is adsorbed there is no change in composition. It is possible and sometimes beneficial to practice meditation while engaged in another activity such as yoga or Pilates, and even martial arts. You can also practice your breathing. When stretching hold it if possible closing your eyes and tolerating the discomfort while learning to relax the rest of your body. Breathe slow/ long and deep until the discomfort dissipates. Slowly moving from one position to another.

Meditation can be practised anywhere, at any time and in any position that you find comfortable in. Any length of time but the more focused you can become the more beneficial you will be. Meditation is very effective when dealing with difficult situations and overcoming our shortcomings and bad habits and/or addictions.

People are "unfree" because of the "horrid instincts" school of thought. At the heart of this un-freedom is cruelty/ evil and inequality. The division of property, in this case money. There is a great divide between the rich and the poor. The rich want a better quality of life and as much life as their money will buy, but the poor constantly remind them they are still mortal. Whether a person is considered rich or poor by "others" does not mean the person is. Ultimately it is internally driven/ a psychological decision of the individual. How do they feel about it? It is a state of mind.

If we were instinctively evil there would be no hope. However this is not the case , we are however "substitutive" evil. Therefore we have 2 choices A) to recognize and overcome, or B) submit and be destroyed and or consumed. A "substitute" by definition is "a person or thing that can take the place of another. That other is love." We may be "inherently evil" but we are not incorrigible, meaning we also do have the ability to learn. This learning does however come at a price, that price being pain/ isolation and even having our lives inconveniently interrupted.

Evil is necessary to prove Gods ultimate superiority. "thy will be done"

The bible may attempt to explain in its' first book of Moses called Genesis the story about and Adam and Eve. I like to think of it as the awakening of humankind. Regarding the boundaries of the self and emersion of the ego from the subconscious. The fear of God is the beginning of wisdom. Although we have invented these boundaries that enslave us we also like to test them. In doing so we move them over time farther and farther from the original purpose they were designed for until they become meaningless.

Man has been searching for God for so long we have failed as a species to recognize the signs provided that we have also wandered away from him. We have become lost in our quest.. It is what we call "faith" that matters now, Not the literal seeing with the eyes but spiritual vision.

It has been said that everyman intuits that they are God. This intuition is corrupted by applying it to the "self" and he will then do whatever is necessary to confirm that distorted illusion. Through substitute seeking and substitute sacrifices he propels himself through the ocean of other equally driven souls, and the violent friction of these overlapping ego's (selfish ambition)sparks the nightmare we call "history".

All we really want is unity/ peace and a sense of community, but this means death to ourselves (inner self). By choosing to keep it alive and in doing so we struggle through our existence whether we want to or not. In order to avoid this instantaneousness of death, people choose to kill themselves, slowly over time. We do this through addictions etc. In an effort to preserve ourselves.

I ask you for what? and what are you afraid of? being forgotten/ remembered?

Politically this view that inequality and social injustice are inevitable and as the population increases by various factors such as immigration and pro-creation and even migration this percentage will stay the same however the number it represents will increase.

ENTROPY- the amount of disorder in a closed system can only increase in direct proportion to the amount of increase contained within the system. Entropy like a black hole can only increase.
If this be the case then there can be no amount of social reform, save a Marxist revolution.

HABITS

HABITS AS we have come to understand them are nothing more than an addictive behaviour. Society has spent a great deal of money and time studying the subject of these addictive behaviours and their treatment. The medical society even calls some of these addictions diseases. Addictions describe an individual's particular habit or "coping mechanism" regarding a specific behaviour. Behaviour can be described using various terms such as good/ bad/ appropriate/ automatic/mechanistic/ impulsive and can also be described as ritualistic. Behaviour also contains within it many habits. Therefore, many habits are what make up an individual's behavior. The Christian bible states this in LUKE 6:45. A good man brings good things out of the good stored up in his heart, and an evil man brings evil things out of the evil stored up in his heart. For the mouth speaks what the heart is full of.

The habits of some may also be funny! Some have even been known to wear their habits. Some habits are good habits such as breathing/ eating/ sleeping/ thinking/and some habits are not so good such as smoking/ alcoholism/ substance abuse/ self-loathing. Auctions are a good example of "impulse buying"

Many recovering/ recovered addicts have been made aware of the fact that they needed to accept this change in habits because it was in their best interest.

Changing habitual behaviour is like allowing part of our selves to die, and as we have discussed people are generally afraid to die. This is what makes the process much more difficult. People are by nature resistant to change; this is another example of fear because it includes the "other" as well as the "unknown". Once a person becomes aware and comfortable with the other then they can tweak their behaviour to accommodate it. Sometimes we are always changing to accommodate the "other". These habits do not discriminate and are not exclusive to a certain economic class or race of people.

My first booklet could have been a book for physical weight loss but instead was designed for spiritual weight loss. In other words the letting go of the unimportant and the acquisition and hanging on to things that are.   This change also does not necessarily have to be a welcome change it can also be thrust upon us. When change is thrust upon us and a person does not want to change or is not ready to accept this change then it makes the recovery process much harder. Having said that you now need to ask yourself are you ready to accept this change? Many habits make up our behaviour. Habits as we understand them are made up of three parts;

TRIGGERS or BUTTONS

BEHAVIOUR

REWARD or PUNISHMENT.

The "life cycle" of any habit whether it be good or bad also seems to exist in the physical/ conscious and unconscious mind. Habits can also be described as automatic/ mechanistic/ even ritualistic.
Overcoming bad habits and/or addictions can be dealt with in the same way once we realize that they all exist in the mind. These habits along with our behaviour are also known as idiosyncrasies.

Both habits and addictions are the same thing with different meanings. Both are "coping mechanisms" and both share in the same life-cycle, and that is a trigger/ behavior and either a benefit or reward system. We tend to label them by their final result, where a habit can be either an addiction which is more often than not viewed as negative or as a punishment, and a habit which is not.

An addiction is also classified as an individual's inability to escape, they give in or give up the fight and the cycle starts all over again. This is their coping mechanism and this is how they feel they must deal with their anxieties of their daily life. I had the same difficulties when I quit smoking and/or alcoholism and even homelessness for example.

65

Habits/ addictions exhibit their parasitic existence by using the host's (addicts) immune system to gain control over their mind through pain and discomfort. The use of drugs minimizes this pain and discomfort and over time the host (addict) also becomes resistant to it requiring a higher dose of medication or in some case a change completely. This does run the risk of overdose of the host and this is what is the end game of these habits/ addictions are?

When we practise our habits, in this case addiction(s) we give rise to the potential feelings of regret and envy. This is especially true if we are trying to overcome this(ese) addiction(s). Addictions can be thought of as the proverbial "double edged sword". You regret having practised it and are envious of those who have overcome. Consider an addict who tends to minimize the importance of being clean and/or sober can be said to be experiencing envy. This is because are not only jealous of it but they don't want you to have it either. False prophets and evil spirits are envious of others ability to obtain true enlightenment also pursue this wisdom so much so that they build myths and use fear to discourage others from seeking the truth. Not unlike the "wicked witch" in the "Wizard of Oz" she was green with envy! Is it a reward we seek or is it a punishment?

Also the feeling of boredom can in its own way influence or enable us to participate in various activities we otherwise might not. People seem to do many things for a variety of reasons they are unsure of. For instance people eat for reasons other than nourishment such as: smell/ taste/ texture/anticipation/bored/angry/ depressed/sport/power of suggestion.

Originally published in 1989 with my first booklet titled "The Behavioural System for Weight Loss" my theory turned working model goes;

CAUSE
MOTIVATION
BEHAVIOUR
GOAL

Consider for a moment; **REFLEX/ BREATHING/ EATING/ ALCOHOL/ DRUGS/ SMOKING**... all of these are either natural biological functions or are conscious or unconscious responses to internal stimuli, such as the associated pain and discomfort experienced by the withdrawal symptoms or "coping mechanisms".

A lot of personal habits whether they be good or bad arising out of ones need to belong. This too is an unconscious decision to the "inferiority complex". This can also be the result of "peer pressure" and even "rumour". Rumour can also be irrational/ rational and can be very unwise to the one creating or even participating in the spreading of such unfounded accusations. We have also heard about what spreading of gossip can do in the Christian bible EXODUS 20:16.

Boredom needs to be recognized and dealt with effectively because it is everywhere and many things are boring. Even that new job or career you have engaged in has the potential to become boring once the learning curve and nuances have been dealt with. Failure to recognize and deal effectively with boredom can lead us to complacency. When we become complacent then motivation will suffer.

Another problem with chronic boredom and complacency is that a part of our personality known as the super-ego may get involved. When our super-ego gets involved it has a tendency to assume control leading us into high risk behaviour and activities we may not otherwise participate in.

CAUSE/MOTIVATION/BEHAVIOUR/GOAL

What causes Cause? Fear causes Cause! Fear comes in many forms such as greed/ envy/ jealousy and all can also be easily influenced by another primal emotion called anger.

What causes Fear? Well the "other" and/or "the "unknown" causes Fear.

We fear the unknown because we do not understand it. Where there is the "unknown" and the "other" there is also fear.

The gift of fear is "intuition"

The psychologist Abraham Maslow published his theory on behaviour titled "**MASLOW'S HIERARCHY OF NEEDS**" some even called it "**MASLOW'S HIERARCHY OF MOTIVATION**". This "hierarchy" consists of five levels or steps ranging from the "basic to the "self-actualization" and they are arranged as follows;

BASIC NEEDS; consist of; food/ water/ shelter/ clothing/ sex.
Once these "needs" have been satisfied a person can then go to level two.
SAFETY; which means a person should feel more at ease about themselves and will look to gain more by way of employment or securing some sort of income to sustain themselves where they are. Even the "cave man" had to secure assets.
The next step after safety is **BELONGINESS**; this means that a person feels like they belong even if only temporary whether this is in their employment/situation or even in their "community".
The step following this is the **SELF-ESTEEM** level.
SELF-ESTEEM; this is of course where you feel good about where you are and are comfortable. Some people decide to stay at this level never realizing that there is one more level. That level would be the level of
SELF-ACTUALIZATION; this is the level at which you can appreciate that you have really gone through the steps and have accomplished something of value, and this does not necessarily mean for money. Overcoming an addiction would put a person on this level.

When this happens you are said to be at the top of the ladder. It is not uncommon for a person to go on to accomplish more or even to bounce between the last two steps. Yes, it is possible for a person to move from one level to another, however, this would present the person with what is known as being rather unstable such as trying to hold on to a job/ career or a place to live. It can be done, but the person cannot fully appreciate the higher level if they are in fact unstable and not consciously ready for it. Also a person can go backwards on this ladder rather quickly. This is usually the result of economics and when this happens it can be a rather emotionally challenging situation and yes, this to happened to me. aka an "emotional roller-coaster".

BEHAVIOUR

BEHAVIOUR AS we understand it can be described using various adjectives such as; automatic/ mechanistic/ impulsive/ ritualistic. This means that much of our behaviour dwells in our unconscious mind and we sometimes behave in a manner we were not aware of. Behaviour can also be a non-verbal form of communication known as body language.

Because our behaviour is "mechanistic" does not mean that we are a bunch of "humanoids" or "automatons" it simply means that much of our behaviour is predictable. Behaviour can also be "impulsive" or even a natural biological function or a "coping mechanism".

You need to get excited about yourself and anticipate or create change when a healthier/ happier/ more energetic you awaits. It is through behaviour that we "teach" others how we want to be treated. Exercising and eating healthier will help bring about this change. Once you feel better about yourself setting goals that will help you sustain this change will improve and so will your decision making process, yes it is a process. When we set goals they always seem to be a conscious decision to improve our present "self". This book was put together to assist you in accomplishing this. Advancing towards your goals and achieving them is a conscious reminder that you have been or are doing the rights things necessary. This also includes overcoming bad habits/ addictions, although results may vary. Some people may find it necessary to seek professional advice and in no way does this system claim to replace that of a medical professional. Past behaviour does not necessarily predict or dictate future behaviour, and I am sure we have all heard the cliché' "actions speak louder than words". They do!

Behaviour is an observable response to an external stimulus (CAUSE) and also to internal needs (MOTIVATION).
Behaviour is caused by conditions or situations outside the individual. Behaviour is motivated by forces internal to the individual. BEHAVIOUR IS ALWAYS GOAL DIRECTED. Believe it or not behaviour is a verb and as such is 80% non-verbal. aka body language. Listening is another type of behaviour. We also need to practise listening to that which makes no noise. Eating is supposed to be a non-verbal form of communication. Even the clothes you wear can form up to 40% of a good first impression.

CAUSE
MOTIVATION
BEHAVIOUR
GOAL

CAUSE – OVER WEIGHT
MOTIVATION – TO BECOME HEALTHIER
BEHAVIOUR – MORE HEALTH CONSCOUS CHOICES
GOAL – WEIGHT LOSS

Please feel free to personalize and substitute your own goals and objectives.

MOTIVATION: is internally driven by the individual and stems from the enjoyment of the activity you are engaged in. Changing behaviour whether individual or collective is hard work because people will want to know why change is necessary. I believe behaviour is brought about by how we interpret the cause. That is to say that because the cause is an external source we need to internalize this and motivate ourselves toward the appropriate behaviour. This behaviour will propel towards the goal. More often than not we do not dress for success we behave ourselves there first. This cause can also originate in our own internal dialogue.

In our attempt to solve this unknown is what causes a stir in a part of our personalities called the "id". This primitive portion of our personalities is instinctive/ impulsive and demanding immediate attention/

73

satisfaction. It has been likened to the "me first" attitude. The ego develops in response to this impulsive behaviour to keep it in check and anchored in reality. Lastly our super-ego has two parts, however it is beyond the scope of this book to delve in and explain each part and how they work together to complete and form your personality. This is why I recommend participants engage in obtaining a personality profile through their medical/ psychological professional.

There is a part of our super-ego that also tries to keep our ego centered in reality. If this part of our personality is unsuccessful then our internal dialogue will become confused. This will result in their competing with each other and in its attempt to get the ego under control the super-ego assumes control. This happens often when people are "under the influence". The next time you experience this pay attention to your own lack of "impulse control".

When we participate in several bad habits or addictions our super-ego becomes more apparent. I too have experienced this phenomenon. It is easy to spot a super-ego at a hockey or football game, even the "World Series" has culprits. They aren't called super fans for nothing. More importantly are we rewarding ourselves/ others or are we punishing ourselves with this type of behaviour? I believe the latter is true more often than not and the way you can find out is by asking yourself how do you feel about the experience? If you are not truly satisfied then perhaps it is more punishment than reward.

Because this book is concerned with goal setting and overcoming bad habits/ addictions I feel it is important to let you know that when you are "under the influence" your super-ego will let you know that it is in charge now. That is not to say that many a great thing has not happened as a result of someone letting their super-ego be in charge. Sometimes it is necessary to dream big and pursue your passions. When you do, refer to the 3'D's I have included for you on page 6.

Another important tool for you to consider is your unconscious "coping mechanisms". The more you have in your tool box the better off you will be in coping with the life situations as they present themselves and in resolving your conflicting internal dialogue.

Once we begin to process that what we hear whether that be internal or external our "id" being both intuitive and instinctive will naturally lead us to our ego which is also primitive. The need for further evaluation is what leads us to our super-ego. We confirm with the super-ego through our belief system. The only way known to stop this process from occurring is through the death of the physical "self". In other words this process will not stop as long as we are alive and kicking. Once we have confirmed with our belief system we begin to exhibit a corresponding emotion and attitude.

These final three steps in the process is when our behaviour becomes observable caused by conditions or situations external from the individual and forces internal to the individual.

HEAR
SPEAK
FEEL
BELIEF SYSTEM
EMOTION
ATTITUDE
BEHAVIOUR

HEAR: This step usually takes place outside the individual but can also be located within our "internal dialogue".

SPEAK: This step usually follows the first and also originates within our "internal dialogue".

FEEL: This step naturally follows the previous two and is a natural biological function in response.

BELIEF SYSTEM: It is at this step that we evaluate/ process and confirm the previous steps deciding how to or not respond/ react.

EMOTION: Depending on how to or not / react determines whether this step is negative or positive.

ATTITUDE: A negative or positive result at this step would correspond to a negative or positive at the previous step.

BEHAVIOUR: Because behaviour is observable this step is in accordance to the results of the previous two steps. A negative confirmation at the belief system stage would lead the following steps to also be negative. If there was a positive confirmation at the belief system stage then the following three steps would be also.

All behavior seems to be the end result of the four step goal setting function. These functions are described below and exists in either your conscious or unconscious mind. The specific goal has to do with how we feel about it, meaning by achieving it will it make us feel better/ worse than our present self. It is the way humankind copes with their inherent "the inferiority complex". Not only is human nature selfish but when you also consider the "inferiority complex" as identified by Dr. Alfred Adler I believe it answers a lot of not yet asked questions.

Aggression is an irrational and observable, overcompensating for the inherent "inferiority Complex"

CAUSE/MOTIVATION/BEHAVIOUR/GOAL

CREATE A BELIEF IN THE THEORY, THE FACTS WILL CREATE THEMSELVES
Albert Einstein

Detecting the hidden motives in everyday behavior/body language is congenial to a scheme of character reading. Characterology has been around since before Theophrastus and is among the persistent purposes of psychology. "Know thy hidden self"/ "Familiarity breeds contempt"/ "Believe it and prove it in your own person and you shall be saved Sigmund Freud.

The victors always seem to write the history.

"WHAT IS HISTORY, BUT A FABLE AGREED UPON"
Napoleon Bonaparte

Symbolism and the creative impulse are themselves a problem in psychology, subject to psychoanalytic interpretation. Through the ages the sub-conscious has expressed itself pictorially: symbolism in painting is as ancient as literature, in religious symbolism the canvas popularized the doctrine. Paintings literature as well as music can be subjected to psycho-analyzation activity.

This becomes recourse to fantasy in an escape from the too rigid demands of the reality principle.

Symbolism has been with us since the beginning. The philosopher Plato recognized its importance as did the prophets Daniel and Ezekiel as well as Kings such as Solomon/ Nebuchadnezzar as well as others such as Sigmund Freud also recognized the importance of symbols in our subconscious/ conscious mind as did Dr. C.G. Jung another prominent psychologist who made breakthroughs regarding personality types and also studied under Sigmund Freud.

We as humankind have many inherent qualities, if you will, and one of the most prominent ones is known as the "inferiority complex." This was identified by the late Dr. Adler. In order to deal effectively and positively with this "inferiority complex" we need to as individuals devise various "coping mechanisms" that will enable us to achieve the desired outcome (goal), whatever that may be. Human nature is selfish we fight for breath/water/food/safety/ security/ peace/life. We fear death/ pain/anxiety/worry/unknown/psychologically ready/ circle of life / death. Death of the self.

People show their vulnerability inferiority complex by "upping the ante"/ using bigger words/ challenges and we should all know by now what competition does and what personality type it is associated with. Overcome and defeat the "inferiority complex" with confidence/ ability/ love/ thankfulness for the ability because many are not able to defeat it. They have learned to be happy in spite of it, they neither proud nor angry.

Maslow's Hierarchy of Needs could also be based on humankinds climb out of the sub-conscious along with all the privilege/ perils that come with it, and not necessarily based strictly upon the individual. Money and privilege seem to go together and apparently work minimizes any perils it may encounter unequally. Some may call this "Maslow's Hierarchy of Motivation". I will explain this in more detail throughout the book.

To gain insight as to who we are through a personality profile would allow us to become more knowledgeable as to the whole and where we should fit in society. Also we may be able to put a stop to being driven by impulses we do not understand. Everyone should be psychoanalyzed. For in doing so would hopefully discover their hidden self and gain a deeper and substantial understanding of themselves. Western man seems to be ego and thing bound whereas eastern man is not.

Using the four steps described above will enable you to overcome these counter-productive coping mechanisms and replace them with more appropriate ones. A person cannot escape the fact that we as human beings are going to have good/bad habits throughout our time on this planet. The trick is to have them benefit us rather than punish and hinder our progress. Rewards can also be celebratory and/or even mundane.

I am a spiritual person and a strong believer in God. There are believers both male and female who believe they must participate in and are required to practice "corporal mortification" upon themselves in cases like these behaviours can become ritualistic and even addictive. I do not subscribe to this ritualistic behaviour.

Alcohol- al-kuhl (originally Arabic)

Alcoholism/ drug abuse/ diabetes are in my opinion all part of our over-indulging. We are over-compensating for our "inferiority complex" using a faulty "coping mechanism" I also believe they are preventable and if they are in fact preventable are they really diseases or just a bad habit? Self-awareness and self-control may be the answer as well as the government and society getting more involved. I have met many that where using both drugs and alcohol to cope with stresses originating by the lack of affordable housing. It seems to be a   crisis many of us seem to be faced with today. Housing along with food/ water/ clothing are all part of a human beings "Basic needs". Without these basic needs being met an individual's mental health suffers and as a result puts added stresses on the very society that it is supposed to help.

Discipline to can be a form of punishment.   What is the end goal? It may be designed to teach/instruct as to how one ought to behave/perform.

Anticipation/ trigger/ craving/behavior/ reward or punishment? Where/ what is the benefit?
Physical and/or psychological habit/ addiction/ pattern of behavior ultimately leading one to reward or punishment/ Meditation
Because habits are behaviours known as idiosyncrasies this would also make them "mechanistic."

What is the difference between an addiction and a habit? A reward and punishment? What is there purpose?   Benefit or reward? What is it designed to do? Is it negative reinforcement designed to get a positive result? To somehow gain enlightenment/ Atonement/ Self-loathing? Is it possible to turn this negative reinforcement into a reward? Was Pavlov successful? Believe it or not the answer is yes. It does however depend on your perception and requires the understanding of others. As stated earlier we are all part of the whole. This has also been agreed upon by Albert Einstein who stated "it is the removal of the optical delusion that we are separate individuals set off from the whole", Albert Einstein is also quoted as saying "keep it simple, but not too simple".

Both habits and addictions are the same thing with different meanings. Both are "coping mechanisms" and both share in the same life-cycle, and that is a trigger/ behavior and either a benefit or reward system. We tend to label them by their final result, where a habit can be either an addiction which is more often than not viewed as negative or as a punishment, and a habit which is not. An addiction is also classified as an individual's inability to escape, they give in or give up the fight and the cycle starts all over again. This is their coping mechanism and this is how they feel they must deal with the stresses of their daily life. I had the same difficulties when I quit smoking and/or alcoholism and even homelessness for example. Habits/ addictions exhibit their parasitic existence by using the host's (addicts) immune system to gain control over their mind through pain and discomfort. The use of drugs minimizes this pain and discomfort and over time the host (addict) also becomes resistant to it requiring a higher dose of medication or in some case a change completely. This does run the risk of overdose of the host and this is what is the end game of these habits/ addictions are?

In addition to all these mechanistic / impulsive and ritualistic behaviours there is also the social stigma attached to them. The word stigma by definition is a mark against your reputation. This new fear produces superstition and does not promote religion. Stigma usually originates with someone of low self-esteem who is also unconsciously dealing effectively with their "inferiority complex" because they are trying to bring you down to their level. Inferiority complex and behavior habits we need recovery from and also some sort of religious experience, otherwise we have been known to kill ourselves slowly over time and in varying degrees. To overcome these not so good habits we need to dissociate them. This means to come to the realization that we have ranked them higher than they ought. We have done this consciously and we rationalized the process. We also did this as a means of belonging to a group in order to gain companionship or friendship. A group that does not/ did not exist. In reality it was nothing more than a collection of individuals pursuing their own goals and objectives. It is the habit of thinking that must be changed. A good of mine calls it "stinkin' thinkin'" because alcohol was/is my drug of choice and AA had nothing to do with my recovery. I don't believe in AA, I also believe every person has the ability to change if they want to. As I have explained this change must first be a conscious choice/ goal or an objective and be pursued whenever and wherever possible until it to becomes mechanistic and dwells in the unconscious.

Symbolism and the creative impulse are themselves a problem in psychology, subject to psychoanalytic interpretation. Through the ages the sub-conscious has expressed itself pictorially: symbolism in painting is as ancient as literature, in religious symbolism the canvas popularized the doctrine. Paintings literature as well as music can be subjected to psycho-analyzation activity.

The thought process of these behaviours/ habits may be frequent but they are also brief. When you see/ feel one coming, stop and acknowledge it then quickly think/do something that will help you to forget about it. Association/dissociation.
Habits can also refer to the collective of our society. We as humans seem to enjoy being oppressed. We for centuries have demanded oppression through elected officials. This is as a substitute for the invisible liberator (God). To be oppressed is the easy way out. Our taxes become a substitute for tithes and we become obedient. It has been said that a slave is in love with their chains. This is another example of a "coping mechanism" that seems to exist in our "unconscious mind". As human beings we prefer to have a visible God

figure such as Kings and Queens and Popes. Faith is ...
Mother Nature was visible to the magical mind. We
elect leaders to oppress us and are happy in our chains.
We do this because as humankind we require a visible
"godlike" leader.

Pertinent psychological principle reads: This origin I now
believe to be the psychological need to have a visible
"god figure" As long as we believe it is not us, it must be
someone else (hero worship). Therefore we must keep
looking for and submitting to the one with the shiniest
sword. A leader whether they be a King, Queen,
President or Prime Minister seems to be our hero and
we will become slaves to heroes both psychotically and
politically. Do we as a people also possess an unresolved
"separation anxiety". Our need for the visible vs
invisible.

Because mechanistic behavior is rooted in the
sub-conscious mind means we are able to practice these
patterns of behavior unconsciously. This means simply
without our knowledge. Have you ever found yourself
eating/ drinking/ smoking our doing something else
without even giving it a thought? We all have. We are all
human and there is nothing wrong until it causes you or
someone else grief. We at times attempt to rationalize
this behavior by saying "because I can" or "oh well, here
we go again". Have you ever stopped yourself and asked
yourself why? Well to explain I will use a habit we all
participate in "eating". We as you know all have to eat.
Many of now eat for reasons other than for

nourishment. Buddha said "if you are hungry ...eat". Many of us eat for reasons other than hunger such as; ...., Smell can even trigger eating as can sound and taste.   Some people claim to sleep better with a full stomach. I also find this statement to be true. The problem with this is it does cause us much unnecessary weight gain and in today's world we do not need any help in that department.

GLOBESITY is a term now known to describe how a basic human need has gotten out of control. Have you ever considered the fact that boredom is a state of mind we all share? Boredom seems to have its' own attitude/ facial expression and behaviours. At times we may feel like the victim and not the agent of such behavior. We also feel these compulsions strongly but are ignorant of the provenance. Would it help to find out it lies somewhere within your "unconscious" mind? How are we going to fix/ change it? Where does this mechanistic behavior originate?

The marketing industry spends millions of dollars trying to invoke visceral responses such as jealousy/ fear/ happiness resulting in those impulse purchases so many people have fallen victim to. What they are really trying to sell you is the dream. A dream of something you don't yet or may never have. When impulse purchases are made they are also usually returned rather quickly, but those marketing companies just don't let up trying

to tap into your subconscious. Gain perspective/ coping mechanisms
Avoid bored/ unhappy= trouble also negative and talkative
As we see ourselves, we have a tendency to see others.
Conflicting and competing thoughts vs. peace of mind
Are we able to transcend the personality?

Even if you were suddenly and unexpectedly enlightened you would still require time to digest and adsorb this new and important information. This very thing is what happened to the disciple of Jesus known as Saul. After his transformation he was referred to as Paul. This period of adjustment is exactly what is supposed to happen, remember "only fools rush in where angels fear to tread".

Whenever we communicate verbally or non-verbally we reveal some and suppress some. We are constantly playing a game with our expressions and our repressions. Certainly little bits of repressed emotion interject with our expressions and betray their source, our unconscious. Attempting to hone ones skill in correctly interpreting non-verbal communication can take an enormous amount of time well invested in oneself. It is extremely important to see more truly, more deeply and more objectively than the untrained mind. Marketing gurus know this and have convinced store keepers to design their stored and decorate them with colour schemes that encourage this impulse. Most of what we buy is on impulse. They depend on it. Impulse is made up of mostly feeding upon the emotion of fear. Think about this for a minute.

I am sure we all know someone who even holds grudges. This kind of behavior is counter-productive. We should share in one another's burdens and we do their successes. People often behave in a manner they understand to be expected and appropriate. Our super ego doesn't make us superhuman even though at times we may feel and think as though we are. Quite often our super ego will assume control after the internal dialogue between the ego has not been resolved. With the super ego in control may result in us getting into trouble with the law more frequently. Also when the super ego is in control and other people are as well, with their own egos and super egos to deal with situations may get a little out of hand. Even though past behavior may be able to predict future behavior the more important issue to understand is the perception of the individual(s).

Only God can read the heart/ mind and determine the "intention" behind the behavior. In the last days, perilous times will come. It seems to me that many people are now just beginning to experience and notice previously unexperienced situations, and a person doesn't need to look hard to find them. Evil seems to be winning this battle, but it is only out of desperation and

can only be short lived. Evil needs to feed upon itself to exist, therefore this too shall end and the meek shall inherit the earth.
The battle between good and evil can only have one logical successor Good.

www.ingramcontent.com/pod-product-compliance
Lightning Source LLC
Chambersburg PA
CBHW041357090426

42739CB00001B/4